THE SLEEPING BEAUTY

PICTURE BOOK

CONTAINING

THE SLEEPING BEAUTY; BLUEBEARD;

THE BABY'S OWN ALAPHABET:

WITH THE ORIGINAL

COLOURED DESIGNS BY

WALTER CRANE

[ZHINGOORA BOOKS]

Long, long ago, in ancient times, there lived a King and Queen,
And for the blessing of a child their longing sore had been:

At last, a little daughter fair, to their great joy, was given,
And to the christening feast they made, they bade the Fairies
seven—

The Fairies seven, who loved the land—that they the child might bless,

Yet one old Fairy they left out, in pure forgetfulness.
And at the feast, the dishes fair were of the reddest gold;
But when the Fairy came, not one for her, so bad and old,
Angry was she, because her place and dish had been forgot,
And angry things she muttered long, and kept her anger hot.

Until the Fairy godmothers their gifts and wishes gave:
She waited long to spoil the gifts, and her revenge to have.
One gave the Princess goodness, and one gave her beauty rare;
One gave her sweetest singing voice; one, gracious mien and air;
One, skill in dancing; one, all cleverness; and then the crone

Came forth, and muttered, angry still, and good gift gave she
none;

But said, that in the future years the Princess young should die,
By pricking of a spindle-point—ah, woeful prophecy!
But now, a kind young Fairy, who had waited to the last,
Stepped forth, and said, "No, she shall sleep till a hundred years
are   past;
And then she shall be wakened by a King's son—truth I tell—
And he will take her for his wife, and all will yet be well."

In vain in all her father's Court the spinning-wheel's forbid
In vain in all the country-side the spindles sharp are hid;
For in a lonely turret high, and up a winding stair,
There lives an ancient woman who still turns her wheel with care.

The Princess found her out one day, and tried to learn to spin;
Alas! the spindle pricked her hand—the charm had entered in!

And down she falls in death-like sleep: they lay her on her bed,
And all around her sink to rest—a palace of the dead!
A hundred years pass—still they sleep, and all around the place
A wood of thorns has risen up—no path a man can trace.
At last, a King's son, in the hunt, asked how long it had stood,
And what old towers were those he saw above the ancient wood.

An aged peasant told of an enchanted palace, where
A sleeping King and Court lay hid, and sleeping Princess fair.
Through the thick wood, that gave him way, and past the thorns
that   drew

Their sharpest points another way, the King's son presses through.
He reached the guard, the court, the hall,—and there, where'er he stept,
He saw the sentinels, and grooms, and courtiers as they slept.

Ladies in act to smile, and pages in attendance wait;
The horses slept within their stalls, the dogs about the gate.

The King's son presses on, into an inner chamber fair,
And sees, laid on a silken bed, a lovely lady there;
So sweet a face, so fair—was never beauty such as this;
He stands—he stoops to gaze—he kneels—he wakes her with a kiss.

He leads her forth: the magic sleep of all the Court is o'er,—
They wake, they move, they talk, they laugh, just as they did of yore
A hundred years ago. The King and Queen awake, and tell
How all has happed, rejoicing much that all has ended well.
They hold the wedding that same day, with mirth and feasting good—
The wedding of the Prince and Sleeping Beauty in the Wood.

---

x

y

w

r

n

b

d

Aa Bb Cc Dd

13

Aa Bb Cc Dd

13

As I was going up Pippin Hill
Pippin hill was dirty.
There I met a pretty miss,
And she dropped me a curtsy.

Boys and girls come out to play.
The moon doth shine as bright as day:
Come with a whoop, come with a call,
Come with a good will, or not at all.

Cuckoo, cherry tree
Come down & tell me
How many years
I have to live!

Ding, dong, bell,
Pussy's in the well.
Who put her in?
Naughty Johnny Green.
Who pulled her out?
Little Tommy Trout.
Little Tommy Trout.

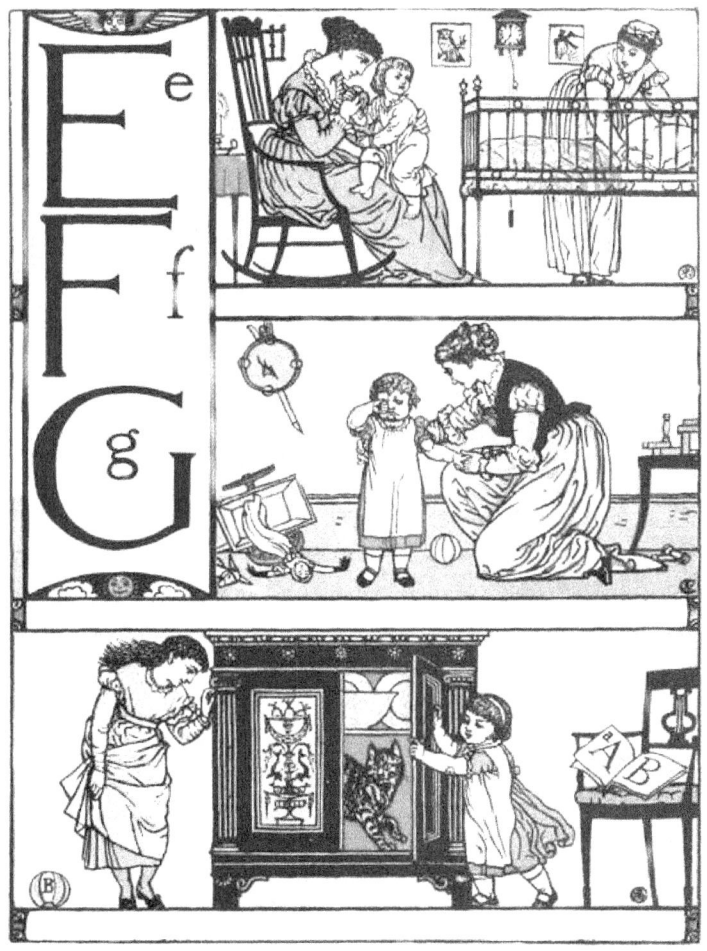

Early to bed, and early to rise,
Is the way to be healthy, wealthy, and wise.

For every evil under the sun
There is a remedy, or there is none.

15

If there be one, try and find it;
If there be none, never mind it.

Great A, little A, Bouncing B,
The cat's in the cupboard.
And she can't see me.

Hark! hark! the dogs do bark,
The Beggars are coming to town.
Some in rags & some in jag's
And some in velvet gowns.

I had a little pony
They called it Dapple Gray,
I lent it to a lady
To ride a mile away.
She whipped it, she slashed it,
She drove it through the mire.
I will not lend my pony more,
For all the ladies' hire.

John Smith, fellow fine,
Can you shoe this horse o' mine?
Yes, indeed, and that I can
As well as any man!
There's a nail upon the tae, &c
To make the powny speel the brae;
There's a nail and there's a brod
—a horse weel shod.

King o' Katchem met a king
In a narrow lane;
Says this king to that king
"Where have you been?"

Oh, I've been a hunting
With my dog & my doe
Pray lend him to me,
That I may do so.

"There's the dog, TAKE the dog."
"What's the dog's name?"
"I've told you already."
"Pray tell me again."

Ladybird, ladybird, fly away home,
Your house is a-fire, your children all gone,
All but one that lies under a stone;
Fly the home, ladybird, ere it be gone!

Multiplication is vexation,
Division is twice as bad;
The Rule of Three it puzzles me
And Fractions drive me mad!

Nievie, nievie, nicknack,
Which hand will ye tak'?
Tak' the right, or tak' the wrong,
I'll beguile ye, if I can.

Oh, Mother, I'm to be married
To Mr. Punchinello,
To Mr. Pun,
To Mr. Chin,
To Mr. Nel,
To Mr. Lo,
Mr. Pun, Mr. Chin, Mr. Nel, Mr. Lo
To Mr. Punchinello.

Pat a cake, pat a cake, baker's man,
Prick it and bake it as fast as you can.
Prick it, and bake it, and mark it with B,
And put it in the oven for baby and me.

Queen of Hearts,
She made some tarts,

All on a summer's day.
The Knave of Hearts,
He stole the tarts,
And took them all away.

Rain, rain,
Go to Spain,
And never come back again.

See, Saw, Margery Daw,
Sold her bed, and lay upon straw.

Three children sliding on the ice,
Upon a summer's day;
As it fell out they all fell in:
The rest they ran away.

Uphill spare me,
Downhill 'ware me,

On level ground spare me not,
And in the stable forget me not.

Valentine

The rose is red; the Violet's blue
The pink is sweet; & so are you.

"We'll go a-shooting," says Robin to Bobbin;
"We'll go a-shooting," says Richard to John.

"We'll go a-shooting," says John all alone;
"We'll go a-shooting," says every one.

Xmas gifts.

The first day of Xmas
My mother sent to me
A partridge in a pear tree.

Yule days.

The king sent his lady on the first Yule day,
A papingo-aye
Who learns my carol & carries it away?

Zoological gardens.

Where you shall go, too;
But it's through A B C that we get to the Zoo.

BLUEBEARD.

Once on a time there lived a man hated by all he knew,
Both that his ways were very bad, and that his beard was blue;
But as he was so rich and grand, and led a merry life,
A lady he contrived at last to induce to be his wife.

For a month after the wedding they lived and had good cheer,
And then said Bluebeard to his wife, "I'll say good-bye, my dear;
Indeed, it is but for six weeks that I shall be away,

I beg that you'll invite your friends, and feast and dance and play;
And all my property I'll leave confided to your care.
Here are the keys of all my chests, there's plenty and to spare."

"But this small key belongs to one small room on the ground-
floor,—
And this you must not open, or you will repent it sore."

And so he went; and all the friends came there from far and wide,
And in her wealth the lady took much happiness and pride;
But in a while this kind of joy grew nearly satisfied.

And oft she saw the closet door, and longed to look inside.
At last she could no more refrain, and turned the little key,
And looked within, and fainted straight the horrid sight to see;
For there upon the floor was blood, and on the walls were wives,
For Bluebeard first had married them, then cut their throats with
knives.

And this poor wife, distracted, picked the key up from the floor,
All stained with blood; and with much fear she shut and locked
the   door.
She tried in vain to clean the key and wash the stain away
With sand and soap,—it was no use. Bluebeard came back that
day;
At once he asked her for the key,—he saw the bloody stain.—

"You have been in the closet once, and you shall go again!"
"O spare me, spare me! give me time, nor kill me hastily!"
"You have a quarter of an hour,—then, madam, you must die!"
"O sister Anne, go up, go up, and look out from the tower;"
"I'm dead unless my brothers come in a quarter of an hour!"
And Anne looked once, and Anne looked twice, and nothing saw abroad,
But shining sun and growing grass, and dust upon the road.

34

"Come down!" cried Bluebeard, "time is up!" With many a sigh and   moan,
She prayed him for a minute more; he shouted still, "Come down!"
"O sister Anne, look out, look out! and do you nothing see?"
"At last I see our brothers two come riding hastily."

"Now spare me, Bluebeard,—spare thy wife!" but as the words were
said,

And just as Bluebeard's cruel blade was descending on her head,
In rushed the brothers with their swords,—they cut the murderer
down,
And saved their sister's life, and gained much glory and renown;

And then they all with gold and plate and jewels rare made free,
And ever after lived content on Bluebeard's property.

The End